Leather on Willow

The Pocket Book of Cricket

Richard Benson

Illustrations by Ian Baker

summersdale

LEATHER ON WILLOW

First published in 2005 with text by Nick Atkinson

This revised and substantially updated edition © Summersdale Publishers Ltd 2012

Illustrations by Ian Baker

Summersdale Publishers Ltd
46 West Street
Chichester
West Sussex
PO19 1RP
UK

www.summersdale.com

Printed and bound in China

ISBN: 978-1-84953-259-4

Substantial discounts on bulk quantities of Summersdale books are available to corporations, professional associations and other organisations. For details contact Summersdale Publishers by telephone: +44 (0) 1243 771107, fax: +44 (0) 1243 786300 or email: nicky@summersdale.com.

To..

From..

Contents

Introduction

Like many other sports established as a national institution, cricket has a place in the hearts of Britons everywhere. However, its distinction lies in its reputation as a gentleman's game; it is steeped in tradition and romantic notions of faultlessly turned-out players in pressed white slacks, beautifully knitted pullovers and schoolboy caps, engaging in concentrated but polite competition – the perfect combination of skill, sportsmanship and civility.

While cricket has more than lived up to this honourable reputation, it has also developed into something that is infinitely more diverse and dynamic – the game is played in the gullies and backstreets of India and Pakistan, on the white sands of the West Indies' coastline and in the ultra-modern stadiums of Australia. Twenty20 and One Day Internationals have brought the game into the realms of prime-time viewing, with high-profile matches being decided in an afternoon's play.

This book collects trivia, quotes, anecdotes and jokes from across the span of cricket's rich history, from W. G. Grace's wind problem to Shane Warne's metrosexual makeover, to remind us that, while the face of the sport may change, some of the best things remain the same – like stony-faced umpires, meticulously groomed pitches and the tack-tock sound of leather on willow.

Even if I knew I was going to die today,
I think I'd still want to hear the
cricket scores.

G. H. Hardy

Creasing Up

'I can't understand it,' said the captain. 'It was such an important game that I bribed the umpire and yet we still lost.'

'Terrible, isn't it,' a bowler agreed. 'It's getting so you can't trust anyone.'

Simply Not Cricket

Despite cricket's obvious British connections, it was not until 1880 – three years after the first official Test match, played in Melbourne – that a Test was played in the United Kingdom, at the Kennington Oval between 6 and 8 September. The match saw a formidable Australian squad facing off against an English team captained by Lord Harris, including the brothers W. G., E. M. and G. F. Grace. Without their star bowler Fred Spofforth, Australia were weakened and in the end England secured the home victory, winning by five wickets.

How's That?

Like many great inventions, cricket has a history which suggests there was no single moment that heralded its arrival – certain theories have it that an early version of the game was played by the children of farming and metal-working communities of the Weald in Kent and Sussex in the 1300s, using a makeshift ball of sheep's wool and a farming implement to strike it. Little did they know that wool would still figure in the game, albeit less tastefully, some 600 years later.

Batting

Cricket is a sport which relies on lightning-fast reaction times: as well as having a keen eye, good coordination and dexterity, a competent batsman should be able to judge the pitch and spin of the ball from the moment it leaves the bowler's hand – no mean feat when faced with a 100-mph cannonball from the likes of Shoaib Akhtar or a wild leg-spinner from Shane Warne. The batsman must strike a balance between defending his wicket, grabbing runs whenever the opportunity arises and attacking the oncoming ball, pouncing from a Zen-like state of readiness into fierce animation.

Gone are the days of posing proudly in front of the wickets with only some pads, a box and a hefty clump of facial hair to protect you while awaiting the next daisy-cutter – today batsmen appear almost warrior-like with their helmet grill and protective gloves. Their 'weapon' – the humble willow bat – has itself undergone an evolution, from something that resembled a caveman's best head-flattener (the earliest example of which dates back to 1729) to the more uniform and elegantly shaped equipment used by the likes of Jack Hobbs in the thirties.

◇◇◇◇◇◇◇◇◇ Simply Not Cricket ◇◇◇◇◇◇◇◇◇

Bhausaheb Nimbalkar of India was on 443 runs with one day to go in a first-class match. He was just nine runs short of the then world record of 452, held by Don Bradman. Unfortunately, Nimbalkar was unable to play on the final day and so missed out on the record – not because of illness or injury, but because he had to put his name to another record: that of his marriage, which was scheduled for the same day.

Creasing Up

A batsman is performing terribly at the crease.
During a lull, he says to the wicket-keeper, 'I bet you've
seen worse players than me.' The wicket-keeper, who has
clearly heard him, doesn't reply. 'I said I bet you've seen
worse players than me!'
'I heard you,' says the wicket-keeper. 'I was
just trying to think.'

It's hard work making batting look effortless.

David Gower

How's That?

 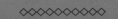

King of concentration and cricket stamina,
Hanif Mohammad once batted for 16 hours and 10
minutes – nearly three full days – against the West Indies,
scoring 337 runs.

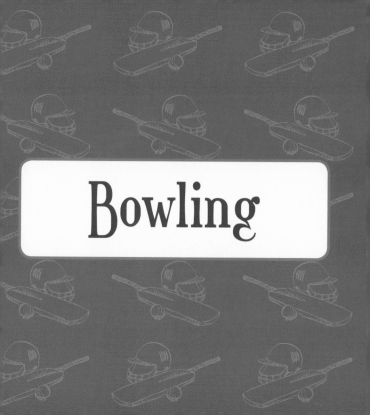

Bowling

Bowling is an area of cricket that has been utterly transformed since its humble beginnings, when it was common for bowlers to deliver the ball along the ground with an underarm pitch or 'daisy-cutter'. This was outlawed when a technique known as 'jerking' (no sniggering, please), enabled bowlers to project the ball at a 'dangerous' pace. Of course, nowadays bowling can be dangerous in the truest sense, with fast-bowlers putting enough power into their deliveries to kill a small horse. Luckily, there is much more to bowling than brute strength, which shows in the sheer variety of bowling techniques used in the modern game.

Some more interesting bowling terms include:

Death bowling – nothing to do with the Grim Reaper, rather this refers to the situation where a bowler from the leading side aims to keep runs to a minimum in the last few overs of short-form cricket matches.

Googly – an odd name for an odd delivery, which sees leg-spin bowlers switch technique (from leg-spin to off-spin) to try to catch their opponent unawares – enough to make anyone's eyes go googly.

Yorker – sounds delicious, but one of these will leave a bad taste in a batsman's mouth with the ball pitched awkwardly at the batsman's feet.

I bowl so slow that if after I have delivered the ball I don't like the look of it, I can run after it and bring it back.

J. M. Barrie

Creasing Up

A bowler's mother was watching proudly from the stand.
Next to her, a spectator turned to his friend.
'He's a good bowler,' he observed, 'but his length varies.'
'Don't be stupid,' interrupted the mother. 'He's five foot
eight, and always has been!'

Simply Not Cricket

Universally recognised as one of the greatest bowlers in the history of the game, Shane Warne was a star of Australian's international team in the nineties and on into the twenty-first century. Warnie was always regarded as a bit of a ladies' man (even during the years he was clearly spending too much time at the barbie), and since his retirement from the international game in 2007 he has undergone what can only be described as a 'metrosexual makeover'; losing weight, radically changing his wardrobe and beginning an exercise and beauty regime. Who says there's no glamour in the game of cricket?

How's That?

The slowest ever recorded bowling took place in New Zealand in 1921. A visiting bowler fell down a concealed manhole as he began his run up towards the crease. It took rescuers a total of 14 hours to free the man and after 14 hours and 11 minutes, the unhurt man delivered the first ball of his over.

Fielding

A fielder's role is to prevent runs being scored by stopping the ball reaching the boundary and by providing fast returns to the wicket to catch the batsman out.

The main weapons in the fielder's armoury are coordination, an accurate throw, alertness over extended periods of play and quick reactions; less crucial skills include nose-picking, scratching, staring into space and the ability to repel even the easiest catch away from one's hands. It may seem like laid-back, uneventful work, but a good fielder can be worth his weight in gold.

Simply Not Cricket

Michael Holding once threw a ball from the boundary, which hit one set of stumps and went on to hit the other set. Although both batsmen were out of their creases at the time, the umpire was too confused to give either of them out.

It is extremely cold here. The England fielders are keeping their hands in pockets between balls.

Christopher Martin-Jenkins, English cricket
commentator and journalist

 ## How's That?

A fielder positioned close to and in front of the batsman
on the on or off side of the pitch is known as a 'Silly Mid
On/Off' – nothing to do with playing the fool, but rather it
refers to the danger factor of the position (for the fielder),
as in 'My, won't I look silly without any front teeth after
this next ball hits me in the chops because I'm standing so
close to the batsman?'

Wicket-Keeping

Wicket-keepers must be ready for action at all times – with the reflexes of a cat and the hands of an exceptionally large frog. Making an acrobatic leap for the ball is a regular demand, though most wicket-keepers will testify that it's not just for the cameras. And then there's the art of the 'run out', where keepers are on the receiving end of lightning throws from fielders in the hope of catching a batsman with his trousers down. Failing all of that, a wicket-keeper should at least try to not take a ball to the face.

As the player closest to the batsman, the wicket-keeper also strives to throw him off his game with 'gentlemanly' comments and quips, which often translates as slandering of the first order; or 'sledging', as it is known.

Keepers often hold the captaincy role because of the unique vantage point they have – modern-day notables include the great Alec Stewart, Aussie Adam Gilchrist and Sri Lankan international Kumar Sangakkara. And let's not forget, wicket-keepers are also often relied on to rack up the runs when it comes to their turn to bat – in this sense they are truly the renaissance men of the game.

How's That?

Alan Knott, Wisden's Cricketer of the Year for 1970 and England and Kent wicket-keeper, was known to put steaks inside his gloves for added protection.

Creasing Up

The captain was looking for new blood for his side, which was struggling miserably. 'OK,' he said to one new member, 'what are you like at wicket-keeping?'

'Passable,' replied the applicant.

'That's no good,' said the captain, 'we've already got one like that. We want one that's impassable!'

I doubt if many of my contemporaries, especially the older ones, did many exercises. I have often tried to picture [Godfrey] Evans and [Denis] Compton doing press-ups in the outfield before the day's play, but so far have failed miserably.

Peter May, former English cricketer

Simply Not Cricket

James Bond creator Ian Fleming was known to have attended Eton with the father of Henry 'Blowers' Blofeld, who in his later years was best known for his well-spoken cricket commentary. Fleming's close connection with old Blowers has given rise to the suggestion that the latter was the inspiration for *Thunderball*'s scar-faced, kitten-petting maniac Ernst Stavro Blofeld.

Equipment

The contemporary game of cricket uses two bats, two sets of stumps, a ball and a vast array of protective gear – however, cricket is played the world over with every kind of makeshift gear imaginable, from home-made bats to driftwood stumps, showing that the desire to play is all that's really necessary to enjoy the sport in its essence.

The cricket bat is nowadays a highly developed tool, but gladly it retains its heritage in being made from ever-reliable willow. Cricket balls, too, are still made from cork and twine with a leather covering and a stitched seam – a deep cherry-red colour is most common, though for Twenty20 games a white ball is used, presumably to ensure it stands out against the often garish colours of the teams' clothing.

As the game becomes more and more dynamic, so too does the protective gear, which may include leg pads, chest pads, thigh pads and forearm pads, not forgetting of course the indispensable 'box'. However, in many fans' minds there is only one piece of kit which is truly essential to look the part on the field, and that's the timeless knitted pullover.

How's That?

The history of groin protection in cricket is, perhaps understandably, not a subject much discussed in writing and records of the game. However, some sources have it that early boxes were shaped from lightweight metal and filled with padding, meaning that if a player were to be struck in the 'nether regions' there was every chance of a distinctive 'chime' emanating from his underpants.

Creasing Up

What's worse than wearing a cold box from
your sports bag?
Wearing a warm box from someone else's.

Simply Not Cricket

Perhaps in a bid to bolster the game's modern image, T20 strip designers seem to go to town when deciding on colours: Surrey CCC's 2011 strip consisted of a dayglo green top with black trousers, perhaps following the lead of Australia's equally garish orange-gold and grey ensemble in 2008. Middlesex CCC have even enjoyed a snazzy hot-pink outfit – all of which have brought colour to the world of Twenty20.

Rules

The rules and strange names used in cricket may seem incomprehensible to those who don't have an in-depth knowledge of the game, but they have a long and interesting history. The first organisation to come anywhere near to enforcing universal rules for cricket was Marylebone Cricket Club in 1788, when it produced its Code of Laws.

But where would rules be without their enforcers? Sheriff of play on the cricket pitch is of course the umpire – calm, collected, eagle-eyed – an all-knowing adjudicator and guardian of bowlers' jumpers.

Although usually known for their impartial and unemotional manner, certain umpires have written themselves into the history of the game – such as the charming Dickie Bird, and David 'Shep' Shepherd – proving that there's more to them than an encyclopedic knowledge of the rules.

Here are some of the more 'colourful' examples of cricket rules and terminology:

LBW – of course this usually signifies 'Leg Before Wicket', but in one match against Australia it was more a case of 'Shoulder Before Wicket' for Sachin Tendulkar. He was controversially given out LBW as he crouched to avoid the bounce of a fast bowl, bending low enough for his shoulder to obstruct the ball's path to the wickets.

Handling the ball – a batsman deliberately using his padded hand to direct the ball away from the stumps. This occurred in the England–Australia Test in 1993 when Graham Gooch jabbed the ball away from the wickets, after playing a defensive shot that bounced behind the crease – perhaps he was keen to brush up on his boxing skills?

Caught – though this is one of the more regular ways a batsman can end his spell, sometimes things can get weird – take, for instance, the time Aussie Andrew Symonds was given out caught in a match against Sri Lanka, where his straight drive rebounded off teammate Michael Clarke's thigh pad, while at the bowler's end, and into the waiting hands of Chaminda Vaas.

Triggered – this has nothing to do with Del Boy's dim-witted friend; rather it refers to an instance where an umpire has hastily and incorrectly given a player out – a trigger-finger reaction maybe?

Creasing Up

How does an umpire check that the bails
are the correct weight?
He takes them to the bail-weigh station.

How's That?

Among the many celebrated names uttered in the umpire Hall of Fame, one is always sure to be heard over the rest: Dickie Bird. As well as being a first-class umpire, he was an unforgettable personality on the pitch who, after retiring, found time to write a best-selling autobiography and even appeared in an episode of the off-the-wall set-up show *Trigger Happy TV*. His grinning visage and eccentric personality were immortalised in a statue erected in Barnsley in 2009. He received an OBE in 2012 for services to his sport and to charity.

Sometimes, people think it's like polo, played on horseback, and I remember one guy thought it was a game involving insects.

Clayton Lambert, West Indian cricketer, on Americans' views of cricket

Etiquette

The 'long walk' to or from the pavilion can be one of cricket's most sobering journeys. When walking out to the crease, the batsman can suffer trepidation and often faces hostility from opposing supporters. An assured walkout from the pavilion can give the impression of courage and anticipated success and intimidate the opposition, whereas displaying one's nerves may instil confidence of victory in the other side.

It is important also to consider the route back from the crease: an unsuccessful spell may cause a batsman to rush swiftly back to the pavilion to contemplate his poor display, whereas a successful batting stint will allow the player to take an elongated stroll, basking in his glory while he does so. This is entirely acceptable, as is stopping en-route to tie and re-tie one's shoelaces in order to enjoy the atmosphere and the applause of the spectators. This and many other unspoken rules regarding good and bad form add to the proceedings of any professional match – it could hardly be called the gentleman's game otherwise…

 ## How's That?

One of the best shaggy-dog stories in cricketing history concerns an unexceptional Middlesex match in 1934, at which one Bradfield J. Archer was found to be in attendance. Archer in particular showed a distinct lack of animation during the proceedings – so much so that it prompted further examination by attendees, who duly discovered that he had in fact passed away in his seat.

Creasing Up

Which cricket team plays while half dressed?
The Vest Indies.

I passed him [Cowdrey] and Bailey as they went in on Friday morning. I murmured 'Good luck'. Cowdrey said 'Thank you, sir'; Bailey said nothing. In five balls Bailey was out and in five hours Cowdrey had made 152. The god of cricket likes good manners.

George Lyttelton, English teacher and essayist, *The Lyttelton Hart-Davis Letters*

Simply Not Cricket

At the Ashes tour of 1932–33 the English team caused a stir with a new bowling tactic known as the 'bodyline' approach. Fielders were placed in short positions backwards of square leg; the ball would be pitched short, to rise at the body of the batsman, causing it to fly off the edge of the bat as the batsman struggled to defend himself, resulting in an easy catch for the awaiting fielders. Following the tour, however, rules against dangerous bowling were introduced and a restriction was placed on the number of fielders permitted backwards of square leg.

The England Cricket Team

The English cricket team was one of the first to be recognised by the Imperial Cricket Conference (later known as the International Cricket Council), yet there were teams claiming to represent England even before Test cricket existed.

In 1739, a team formed under the name 'All-England' to play a match against Kent. The 'national' team was comprised of men from all over the country, excluding Kent. Impressively, 'the unconquerable County' lived up to their moniker and beat the All-England side by 'a very few notches'. Over the next century, records tell of many sides adopting the name 'England' or 'All-England'.

In 1846, William Clarke formed the very grand-sounding 'All-England Eleven', who became the premier touring club in England. As a protest against Clarke's profiteering and undemocratic management style, a breakaway team was formed in 1852 under the even grander-sounding name, 'United All-England Eleven'.

After Clarke's death in 1856, the two sides began playing each other. Their cooperation culminated in a joint tour of North America in 1859; the first overseas cricket tour by any team. Tours of Australia followed, Test cricket was created and the ICC was formed to govern international cricket. Proof that not all in-fighting leads to outright disaster!

How's That?

Those people who are tempted to dismiss cricket as a game that lacks excitement or quirk need look no further than the players themselves to see that this is simply not the case. Cricketers can be thoroughly outrageous and inventive, especially when it comes to their personal image: recall Graham Gooch's absurd handlebar moustache (rivalled only by Merv Hughes' mutant caterpillar), or Beefy's luxurious perm. England's new generation is not without its characters, either – take 'Freddie' Flintoff who, thanks to his surname, has enjoyed associations with everyone's favourite Stone-Age family man Fred Flintstone.

I just want to get into the middle and get the right sort of runs.

Robin Smith, English cricketer, after suffering from diarrhoea on a tour of India

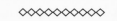 How's That?

The longest recorded throw of a cricket ball was by English bowler Robert Percival in 1882. He managed a throw of 140 yards and 2 feet (or 128.6 metres) at Durham Racecourse, a record that has stood for over 100 years.

◇◇◇◇◇◇◇◇ Simply Not Cricket ◇◇◇◇◇◇◇◇

W. G. Grace was one of the most influential players in the history of cricket, playing first-class cricket for 44 seasons up to 1908, captaining England, and bringing many innovations to the sport. He was extremely competitive, and a great crowd-pleaser.

On one occasion, after being bowled out, he picked up the bail and replaced it on the stump. When questioned by the umpire, he replied ''Twas the wind which took thy bail off, good sir.' The umpire replied 'Indeed, doctor, and let us hope thy wind helps the good doctor on thy journey back to the pavilion.'

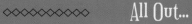

All Out...

Like the game of cricket itself, the England team has had its fair share of ups and downs. However, the fact remains that there is little else so satisfying as seeing a proud England squad end a day's cricket with their heads held high, leaving the Barmy Army eagerly anticipating the next time they'll get to see their boys do battle. And whether they win or lose, players and fans alike can rest assured that, as the New Zealand supporters reminded us with a banner referring to the then-overweight Ian Botham, there's always some good use to be made of English cricketers...

www.summersdale.com